WALKING BASS LINE CONSTRUCTION

PERDIDO

from the *Pathways Towards Greatness* series

by Bob Sinicrope

Sher Music Co.

© 2024 Sher Music Co., P.O. Box 445, Petaluma, CA, 94953 All Rights Reserved.
International Copyright Secured. Made in the U.S.A. No part of this book may be reproduced
in any form without written permission from the publisher.
ISBN – 979-8-9922263-1-7

TABLE OF CONTENTS

About *Walking Bass Line Construction - Perdido and Pathways Towards Greatness* series iii

About the Author iv

Acknowledgements v

Online Hyperlinks Library vi

Chapter 1 Roots - Internalizing Roots 1

Chapter 2 Add the 5th - Internalizing Roots & 5ths 17

Chapter 3 Add the 3rd - Internalizing Root & 3rds 27

Chapter 4 Add the 7th - Internalizing Seventh Chords 35

Chapter 5 One Measure Patterns 40

Chapter 6 More Patterns 49

Chapter 7 Scales 57

Chapter 8 Bass Lines in the Style of 62

        Pops Foster 63

        Walter Page 64

        Milt Hinton 65

        Slam Stewart 66

        Jimmie Blanton 67

        Israel Crosby 68

        George Duvivier 69

        Oscar Pettiford 70

        Percy Heath 71

        Sam Jones 72

        Ray Brown 73

        Red Mitchell 74

        Leroy Vinegar 75

        Andy Simpkins 76

        Paul Chambers 77

        Ron Carter 78

        Charlie Haden 79

        Miroslav Vitous 80

        Bass Line from Backing Track 81

ABOUT WALKING BASS LINE CONSTRUCTION - PERDIDO AND THE PATHWAYS TOWARDS GREATNESS SERIES

Walking Bass Line Construction — Perdido

This book is dedicated to helping bass players at all levels develop walking bass lines with an emphasis on a learn-by-doing approach. Beginners with limited knowledge of how to spell chords and/or who might be new to playing the bass will have an easy pathway to success and be able to quickly function in a group. The backing track options are unique and playing with them will be fun and help you play with a steady pulse. More experienced players will significantly benefit from this thorough approach. The dozens of hyperlinks will offer novel ideas, explanations, enrichment, and inspiration. The final chapter, emulating the styles of some of the greatest walking bass line masters will be of particular interest to advanced players.

Most exercises in this book have a limited range - low E to middle C on the staff. For 4-string traditional tuning electric bass players this means most of the exercises stay within the first 5 frets.

By no means is this method complete, but it is an efficient way to create bass lines without a mastery of playing or theory. Playing these exercises correctly is a start. The goal is to internalize and integrate these bass lines so you can apply them to other tunes. Strive to understand the underlying concepts of each exercise. Make them part of your musical vocabulary.

As useful as these exercises might be, the best way to learn bass lines is to emulate aspects of masterful bass lines you hear on recordings. Have fun and play with confidence and joy.

This book is part of the **Pathways towards Greatness** series. Other **Walking Bass Line Construction** books in the works include *All the Things You Are, Autumn Leaves, Bb Blues, Bb Rhythm Changes, C Minor Blues, F Blues, Satin Doll, So What, Summertime, Sugar* and *Take the A Train*.

— Bob Sinicrope

ABOUT THE AUTHOR

photo by Jamey Aebersold

Bob Sinicrope is a consummate educator. He founded the Milton Academy Jazz Program in 1974 and directed it for 50 years. Winner of several national and international awards, the program produced many fine professional musicians, most notably Aaron Goldberg and Steve Lehman. His students performed at multiple Jazz Education conferences, twice at the White House, the North Sea, Fribourg, Vienne, and Montreux Jazz Festivals. They have played for Eric Alexander, Jim Hall, Dave Holland, Abdullah Ibrahim, Elvin Jones, Steven King, Poncho Sanchez, James Taylor, Desmond Tutu, Kenny Werner, and Victor Wooten and Bass Extremes. Bob's other teaching credits include Jamey Aebersold's Summer Jazz Workshops (40 years), JazzWise Summer School (London, 12 years), and Victor Wooten's Berklee Bass Workshops (7 years). Although Bob has a master's degree in math education, his studies at Berklee College and private lessons with Charlie Banacos, Hal Galper, Rufus Reid, Bob Gullotti, and Mick Goodrick greatly helped him transition to becoming a full-time jazz educator.

Bob was inducted into the *DownBeat Hall of Fame for Jazz Education* in 2024. He was a trustee of the Jazz Education Network (JEN) from 1999-2016 and was President of JEN from 2014-2016. In 2010 Bob received the *National Youth Development Council Service Award* and the *DownBeat Jazz Education Achievement Award*. In 2007, Bob became the inaugural recipient of the *John LaPorta - Jazz Educator of the Year*.

Bob has authored several published magazine articles and wrote a chapter in South African bassist Johnny Dyani's biography *Mbizo-Johnny Dyani*. His **Pathways Towards Greatness** MakeMusic Cloud (SmartMusic) improvisation books are used in 63 countries and his series of **Walking Bass Line Construction** books are published by Sher Music.

Bob has made his mark internationally over the past six decades with clinics in schools and conferences on six continents. In 1972, Bob was commissioned to compose *A Question of Balance* for Jamaica's National Dance Theater Company. Since 1991 his special connections with South Africa began when Abdullah Ibrahim visited Milton Academy and invited the school's combo to tour South Africa. His Milton Academy student groups have toured South Africa more than a dozen times and Bob has taught and performed there many times without his students including directing a week-long workshop for over 100 students at Tshwane University in Pretoria. He also spearheaded the delivery of hundreds of thousands of dollars of donated materials and resources to South African schools and has forged special bonds with many South African township music programs.

A much-in-demand bassist, Bob's credits include performances with Steve Bailey, Shirley Bassey, Jerry Bergonzi, Randy Brecker, Sara Caswell, John Clayton, Jeff Coffin, Billy Eckstine, Bill Evans (saxophone), George Garzone, Aaron Goldberg, Tiny Grimes, Abdullah Ibrahim, Papa Jo Jones, Sean Jones, Mississippi Fred McDowell, Babatunde Olatunji, the Boston Pops, Chris Potter, Rufus Reid, Bobby Sanabria, Kenny Werner, Matt Wilson, Victor Wooten, and the Artie Shaw Band.

Bob can be reached by email at: bob.sinicrope@gmail.com
You can visit his website at: www.bobsinicrope.com

ACKNOWLEDGEMENTS

This method represents the current state of my ongoing learning and understanding of how to help students deepen their ability to freely express themselves in the jazz language. I have been very blessed to have learned from Jamey Aebersold, Christopher Azzara, Steve Bailey, David Baker, Charlie Banacos, Jerry Bergonzi, Gary Burton, Jerry Coker, Hal Crook, Hal Galper, Mick Goodrick, Edwin E. Gordon, Bob Gullotti, Dan Haerle, John LaPorta, Harry Pickens, Herb Pomeroy, Rufus Reid, Kenny Werner and Victor Wooten. These wonderful players/teachers/learners have had a powerful impact on me. Being on the staff of the Aebersold Summer Jazz Workshops for over 40 years, and more recently the Victor Wooten Berklee Bass Weekend Workshop, has provided invaluable enrichment and inspiration.

This project has been greatly enhanced by my editors Eric Goode and Brian Casey. Their advice, keen eyes, perseverance, and encouragement were instrumental in getting this project to completion. John Goldsby was also very helpful with his wisdom, reading and editing. My appreciation also goes to Ted Scalzo for suggesting I share my teachings publicly and for his friendship.

A shout-out also goes to the fine musicians and technicians Mike DiLiddo (guitar and recording), Bobby Floyd (Hammond B3), Barry Lit (drums and recording), Austin Nill (recording), Joel Scanlon (mixing), and Ron Zack (piano) who recorded and/or produced the backing tracks. It was a pleasure for me to play bass with them on these tracks.

My heartfelt thanks to Chuck Sher for his encouragement, significant input, patience and long-standing friendship. It is an honor to be published by Sher Music given their ongoing commitment to jazz education.

Finally, and most significantly, my wife Frances Scanlon has been amazingly helpful with her gifted graphic design skills and editing, and more importantly, her love and support throughout. I thank her for her enthusiasm and commitment to me and this project.

ONLINE HYPERLINKS LIBRARY

This QR code will take you to an **online source of hyperlinks** to various sites that will deepen your understanding of some of the musical concepts presented in **Walking Bass Line Construction – Perdido**.

Each page of exercises has commentary and a title in *underlined* text.

This *underlined* text is an indication that the online source of hyperlinks can help you further your development.

CHAPTER 1

Roots - Internalizing Roots

#1.1

Perdido
Walking Bass Line
Roots - Internalizing Roots

Roots are the foundation of a tune's harmony and the most consonant note in any chord.

Learning to hear the Roots will help you keep your place in the form of the tune.

Sing and play Roots on all tunes to help internalize their sound.

Play with vigor!

To more fully internalize:
1. Listen
2. Sing
3. Play

by Bob Sinicrope

Inspiration, Education, Fun
©2024 SeekingSpirit

WALKING BASS LINE CONSTRUCTION | C Minor Blues

#1.2

Perdido
Walking Bass Line
Roots - Lower Chromatic to Root

Approach Notes are tension notes that resolve to chord tones. They add melodic interest and create rhythmic motion. The resolution is stronger if the Approach Note is on an upbeat and the chord tone is on a downbeat.

This exercise features **Lower Chromatic (LC)** Approach Notes to the **Root (R)**. These work well in bass lines.

Make it dance!

To more fully internalize:
1. Listen
2. Sing
3. Play

by Bob Sinicrope

Inspiration, Education, Fun
©2024 SeekingSpirit

WALKING BASS LINE CONSTRUCTION | C Minor Blues

#1.3

Approach Notes *are tension notes that resolve to chord tones. They add melodic interest and create rhythmic motion. The resolution is stronger if the Approach Note is on an upbeat and the chord tone is on a downbeat.*

This exercise features **Lower Double Chromatic (LD)** *Approach Notes to the* **Root (R)**. *These work well in bass lines.*

Play with spirit!

Perdido
Walking Bass Line
Roots - Lower Double Chromatic to Root

To more fully internalize:
1. Listen
2. Sing
3. Play

by Bob Sinicrope

Inspiration, Education, Fun
©2024 SeekingSpirit

WALKING BASS LINE CONSTRUCTION | C Minor Blues

#1.4

Approach Notes *are tension notes that resolve to chord tones. They add melodic interest and create rhythmic motion. The resolution is stronger if the Approach Note is on an upbeat and the chord tone is on a downbeat.*

This exercise features **Lower Triple Chromatic (LTC)** *Approach Notes to the* **Root (R)**. *These work well in bass lines.*

Play with conviction.

Perdido
Walking Bass Line
Roots - Lower Triple Chromatic to Root

To more fully internalize:
1. Listen
2. Sing
3. Play

by Bob Sinicrope

Inspiration, Education, Fun
©2024 SeekingSpirit

WALKING BASS LINE CONSTRUCTION | C Minor Blues

Perdido
Walking Bass Line
Roots - Upper Double Chromatic to Root

#1.6

Approach Notes are tension notes that resolve to chord tones. They add melodic interest and create rhythmic motion. The resolution is stronger if the Approach Note is on an upbeat and the chord tone is on a downbeat.

This exercise features a **Double Chromatic (UD** *Approach Notes to the* **Root (R)**. These sometimes, but not always work well in bass lines.

Play with zest!

To more fully internalize:
1. Listen
2. Sing
3. Play

by Bob Sinicrope

Inspiration, Education, Fun
©2024 SeekingSpirit

WALKING BASS LINE CONSTRUCTION | C Minor Blues

#1.7

Approach Notes are tension notes that resolve to chord tones. They add melodic interest and create rhythmic motion. The resolution is stronger if the Approach Note is on an upbeat and the chord tone is on a downbeat.

This exercise features **Upper Triple Chromatic (UTC)** approach notes to the **Root (R)**. These do not always work well. Once you learn them, you can choose when you want to use them.

Make your notes ring out!

Perdido
Walking Bass Line
Roots - Upper Triple Chromatic to Root

To more fully internalize:
1. Listen
2. Sing
3. Play

by Bob Sinicrope

WALKING BASS LINE CONSTRUCTION | C Minor Blues

#1.8

Perdido
Walking Bass Line
Roots - Upper Scalar to Root

Approach Notes are tension notes that resolve to chord tones. They add melodic interest and create rhythmic motion. The resolution is stronger if the Approach Note is on an upbeat and the chord tone is on a downbeat.

This exercise features **Upper Scalar (US)** Approach Notes to the **Root (R).**

Make your notes conversational!

To more fully internalize:
1. *Listen*
2. *Sing*
3. *Play*

by Bob Sinicrope

Inspiration, Education, Fun
©2024 SeekingSpirit

WALKING BASS LINE CONSTRUCTION | C Minor Blues

#1.9

Enclosures combine Lower and ***Upper Approach Notes*** *that resolve to chord tones. They add melodic interest and create rhythmic motion.*

*This exercise features **Lower Chromatic (LC)** and **Upper Scalar (US)** approach notes.*

Play with joy!

Perdido
Walking Bass Line
Roots - Enclosure #1
Lower Chromatic - Upper Scalar to Root

To more fully internalize:
1. Listen
2. Sing
3. Play

by Bob Sinicrope

Inspiration, Education, Fun
©2024 SeekingSpirit

WALKING BASS LINE CONSTRUCTION | C Minor Blues

#1.11

Enclosures combine Lower and **Upper Approach Notes** that resolve to chord tones. They add melodic interest and create rhythmic motion.

This exercise features **Lower Chromatic (LC) and Upper Double Chromatic (UD)** approach notes.

It also has **Forward Motion** where the approach notes resolve to a chord tone on a strong downbeat.

Play with expression!

Perdido
Walking Bass Line
Roots - Enclosure #3
Lower Chromatic - Upper Double Chromatic to Root

To more fully internalize:
1. Listen
2. Sing
3. Play

by Bob Sinicrope

Inspiration, Education, Fun
©2024 SeekingSpirit

WALKING BASS LINE CONSTRUCTION | C Minor Blues

Perdido
Walking Bass Line

Roots - Enclosure #4
Upper Double Chromatic - Lower Chromatic to Root

by Bob Sinicrope

#1.12

Enclosures combine Lower *and* **Upper Approach Notes** *that resolve to chord tones. They add melodic interest and create rhythmic motion.*

This exercise features Upper Double Chromatic (UD) *and* **Lower (LC)** *Approach Notes.*

It also has **Forward Motion** *where the Approach Notes resolve to a chord tone on a strong downbeat.*

Make it feel great!

To more fully internalize:
1. Listen
2. Sing
3. Play

Inspiration, Education, Fun
©2024 SeekingSpirit

WALKING BASS LINE CONSTRUCTION | C Minor Blues

#1.13

Perdido
Walking Bass Line
Roots - Enclosure #5
Lower Double Chromatic - Upper Scalar to Root

*Enclosures combine **Lower** and **Upper** Approach Notes that resolve to chord tones. They add melodic interest and create rhythmic motion.*

*This exercise features **Lower Double Chromatics (LD)** and **Upper Scalar (US)** Approach Notes.*

*It also has **Forward Motion** where the Approach Notes resolve to a chord tone on a strong downbeat.*

Play from your heart!

To more fully internalize:
1. *Listen*
2. *Sing*
3. *Play*

by Bob Sinicrope

Inspiration, Education, Fun
©2024 SeekingSpirit

WALKING BASS LINE CONSTRUCTION | C Minor Blues

#1.14

Enclosures combine Lower and Upper Approach Notes *that resolve to chord tones. They add melodic interest and create rhythmic motion.*

This exercise features **Upper Scalar (US) and Lower Double Chromatics (LD)** *Approach Notes.*

It also has **Forward Motion** *where the Approach Notes resolve to a chord tone on a strong downbeat.*

Enjoy your playing!

Perdido
Walking Bass Line
Roots - Enclosure #6
Upper Scalar - Lower Double Chromatic to Root

To more fully internalize:
1. Listen
2. Sing
3. Play

by Bob Sinicrope

Inspiration, Education, Fun
©2024 SeekingSpirit

WALKING BASS LINE CONSTRUCTION | C Minor Blues

#1.15

This exercise incorporates the concepts presented in this chapter. Have fun creating your own bass lines.

Be consistent!

Experiment!

Perdido
Walking Bass Line
Roots - Summary

To more fully internalize:
1. *Listen*
2. *Sing*
3. *Play*

by Bob Sinicrope

Inspiration, Education, Fun
©2024 SeekingSpirit

CHAPTER 2

Add the 5th - Internalizing Roots & 5ths

#2.1

*Bassists frequently utilize **Roots**, **5ths** and **Octaves** in their bass lines. These make a strong harmonic foundation. It's important to become comfortable with these patterns.*

*Sing and play **Roots (R), 5ths (5)** and **Octaves (R̂)** on all tunes to help internalize their sound.*

Play with energy!

Perdido
Walking Bass Line
Add the 5th - Internalizing Roots & 5ths

To more fully internalize:
1. Listen
2. Sing
3. Play

by Bob Sinicrope

Inspiration, Education, Fun
©2024 SeekingSpirit

WALKING BASS LINE CONSTRUCTION | C Minor Blues

#2.3

Bassists frequently utilize Roots, 5ths and Octaves in their bass lines. These make a strong harmonic foundation. It's important to become comfortable with these patterns.

Sing and play **Roots, 5ths and Octaves** on all tunes to help internalize their sound.

Play with confidence!

Perdido
Walking Bass Line
Add the 5th - Internalizing Roots, 5ths and Octaves #2

To more fully internalize:
1. Listen
2. Sing
3. Play

by Bob Sinicrope

Inspiration, Education, Fun
©2024 SeekingSpirit

WALKING BASS LINE CONSTRUCTION | C Minor Blues

Perdido
Walking Bass Line
Add the 5th - Upper Scalar to Root

#2.5

Approach Notes are tension notes that resolve to chord tones. They add melodic interest and create rhythmic motion. The resolution is stronger if the approach note is on an upbeat and the chord tone is on a downbeat.

This exercise features **Upper Scalar (US)** approach notes to the **Root (R)** and **Octave (R̂)**.

Feel the pulse!

To more fully internalize:
1. Listen
2. Sing
3. Play

by Bob Sinicrope

WALKING BASS LINE CONSTRUCTION | C Minor Blues

#2.6

Approach Notes are tension notes that resolve to chord tones. They add melodic interest and create rhythmic motion. The resolution is stronger if the approach note is on an upbeat and the chord tone is on a downbeat.

This exercise features **Lower Chromatic (LC)** approach notes to the **5th (5)**. These work well in bass lines.

Play with a beautiful sound!

Perdido
Walking Bass Line
Add the 5th - Lower Chromatic to 5th

To more fully internalize:
1. Listen
2. Sing
3. Play

by Bob Sinicrope

Inspiration, Education, Fun
©2024 SeekingSpirit

WALKING BASS LINE CONSTRUCTION | C Minor Blues

#2.8

Enclosures combine Lower and Upper Approach Notes that resolve to chord tones. They add melodic interest and create rhythmic motion.

*This exercise features **Lower Chromatic (LC)** and **Upper Scalar (US)** approach notes to the 5th.*

Focus on what you play!

Perdido
Walking Bass Line
Add the 5th - Enclosure

To more fully internalize:
1. *Listen*
2. *Sing*
3. *Play*

by Bob Sinicrope

Inspiration, Education, Fun
©2024 SeekingSpirit

WALKING BASS LINE CONSTRUCTION | C Minor Blues

CHAPTER 3

Add the 3rd - Internalizing Root & 3rds

#3.2

Roots (R or R̂), 3rds (3) and 5ths (5) are the chord tones of triads. Strong bass lines imply the harmony. Chord tones are the most powerful tones to spell out the harmony.

Experiment with your own bass lines with Roots, 3rds and 5ths.

Strive to play without effort!

Perdido
Walking Bass Line
Add the 3rd - Internalizing Triads

To more fully internalize:
1. *Listen*
2. *Sing*
3. *Play*

by Bob Sinicrope

Inspiration, Education, Fun
©2024 SeekingSpirit

WALKING BASS LINE CONSTRUCTION | C Minor Blues

#3.3

Approach Notes *are tension notes that resolve to chord tones. They add melodic interest and create rhythmic motion.*

This exercise features **Lower Chromatic (LC)** *approach notes to the* **3rd (3)**. *These work well in bass lines.*

Be the heartbeat!

Perdido
Walking Bass Line
Add the 3rd - Lower Chromatic to the 3rd

To more fully internalize:
1. *Listen*
2. *Sing*
3. *Play*

by Bob Sinicrope

Inspiration, Education, Fun
©2024 SeekingSpirit

WALKING BASS LINE CONSTRUCTION | C Minor Blues

#3.4

Approach Notes are tension notes that resolve to chord tones. They add melodic interest and create rhythmic motion.

This exercise features **Upper Scalar (US)** approach notes to the **3rd (3)**. They add flavor to your bass line.

Play every note as if it's the most important note you'll ever play!

Perdido
Walking Bass Line
Add the 3rd - Upper Scalar to the 3rd

To more fully internalize:
1. Listen
2. Sing
3. Play

by Bob Sinicrope

Inspiration, Education, Fun
©2024 SeekingSpirit

WALKING BASS LINE CONSTRUCTION | C Minor Blues

#3.5

Approach Notes are tension notes that resolve to chord tones. They add melodic interest and create rhythmic motion. Sometimes these are very effective, but not always. Use your ears to determine when to play them.

This exercise features Lower Double Chromatic (LD) and Upper Double Chormatic (UD) approach notes to the 3rd (3).

Lift up the band!

Perdido
Walking Bass Line
Add the 3rd - Double Chromatic to the 3rd

To more fully internalize:
1. Listen
2. Sing
3. Play

by Bob Sinicrope

Inspiration, Education, Fun
©2024 SeekingSpirit

WALKING BASS LINE CONSTRUCTION | C Minor Blues

#3.7

This exercise incorporates the concepts presented in this chapter. Have fun creating your own bass lines that use Roots, 3rds, Octaves, Lower Chromatics, Upper Scalars, and Enclosures.

Be reliable!

Perdido
Walking Bass Line
Add the 3rd - Summary

To more fully internalize:
1. Listen
2. Sing
3. Play

by Bob Sinicrope

WALKING BASS LINE CONSTRUCTION | C Minor Blues

CHAPTER 4

Add the 7th - Internalizing Seventh Chords

#4.1

Roots (R), 3rds (3), 5ths (5) 7ths (7) and Octaves (R̂) *are the chord tones of the major, minor, dominant, half-diminished and diminished seventh chords. Often a major 6th chord (R356) is used in place of a major 7th chord. Strong bass lines imply the harmony and these tones are the most powerful ones to spell out the harmony.*

Express yourself!

Perdido
Walking Bass Line
Add the 7th - Ingraining Seventh Chords

To more fully internalize:
1. Listen
2. Sing
3. Play

* although the goal of this book is to stay within the 1st 5 frets, this bass line neccesitates making an exception.

by Bob Sinicrope

Inspiration, Education, Fun
©2024 SeekingSpirit

WALKING BASS LINE CONSTRUCTION | C Minor Blues

#4.4

This exercise incorporates the concepts presented in this chapter. Have fun creating your own bass lines that use Roots, 3rds, 5ths, 7ths Octaves, Lower Chromatics, Upper Scalars, and Enclosures.

Bring good energy to the bandstand!

Perdido
Walking Bass Line
Add the 7th - Summary

To more fully internalize:
1. Listen
2. Sing
3. Play

by Bob Sinicrope

Inspiration, Education, Fun
©2024 SeekingSpirit

WALKING BASS LINE CONSTRUCTION | C Minor Blues

CHAPTER 5

One Measure Patterns

#5.1

*A **Passing Tone** is a note between chord tones that connects them. The chord tones are consonant notes and the passing tone creates tension that resolves. Musical 'tension and release' is an important concept that adds interest and motion to your playing.*

Passing Tones *make for strong bass lines.*

Make it Groove!

Perdido
Walking Bass Line
One Measure Patterns - R235 532R

To more fully internalize:
1. *Listen*
2. *Sing*
3. *Play*

by Bob Sinicrope

Inspiration, Education, Fun
©2024 SeekingSpirit

WALKING BASS LINE CONSTRUCTION | C Minor Blues

#5.2

*A **Passing Tone** is a note between chord tones that connects them. The chord tones are consonant notes and the passing tone creates tension that resolves. Musical 'tension and release' is an important concept that adds interest and motion to your playing.*

Passing Tones *make for strong bass lines.*

Drive the Band!

Perdido
Walking Bass Line
One Measure Patterns - R345 543R

To more fully internalize:
1. Listen
2. Sing
3. Play

by Bob Sinicrope

WALKING BASS LINE CONSTRUCTION | C Minor Blues

Inspiration, Education, Fun
©2024 SeekingSpirit

#5.4

The 6th of a chord can usually replace or combine with the major 7th of a chord. The 6th is pretty but less powerful than the major 7th.

*This bass line uses a one measure pattern using the **Root (R), 3rd (3), 6th (6), 5th (5), and Octaves (R̂)**.*

Sing through your bass!

Perdido
Walking Bass Line
One Measure Patterns - R365-R̂653

To more fully internalize:
1. *Listen*
2. *Sing*
3. *Play*

by Bob Sinicrope

Inspiration, Education, Fun
©2024 SeekingSpirit

WALKING BASS LINE CONSTRUCTION | C Minor Blues

#5.5

This bass line uses a one measure pattern using the Root (R), 6th(6), b6 (b6), 5th(5) and Octaves (R̂).

Hear and feel 1/8th note triplet subdivisions when you play 1/4 notes on your bass.

Perdido
Walking Bass Line
One Measure Patterns - R6b65-R̂6b65

To more fully internalize:
1. Listen
2. Sing
3. Play

by Bob Sinicrope

Inspiration, Education, Fun
©2024 SeekingSpirit

WALKING BASS LINE CONSTRUCTION | C Minor Blues

#5.6

This exercise features 2 versions of the pattern **Root** or the **Octave (R or R̂)**, **6th (6), 5th, (5), 6th (6)**. It's often used when playing bass lines in a blues shuffle style.

Learning and internalizing one measure patterns will help you build your own bass lines.

Have fun "digging in" to the sound and feel when playing these bass lines!

Perdido
Walking Bass Line
One Measure Patterns - R656-R̂656

To more fully internalize:
1. Listen
2. Sing
3. Play

by Bob Sinicrope

Inspiration, Education, Fun
©2024 SeekingSpirit

WALKING BASS LINE CONSTRUCTION | C Minor Blues

#5.8

This exercise incorporates the concepts presented in this chapter. Have fun creating your own bass lines that use One Measure Patterns.

Believe in yourself!

Perdido
Walking Bass Line
One Measure Patterns - Summary

To more fully internalize:
1. Listen
2. Sing
3. Play

by Bob Sinicrope

Inspiration, Education, Fun
©2024 SeekingSpirit

WALKING BASS LINE CONSTRUCTION | C Minor Blues

CHAPTER 6

More Patterns

#6.2

*A **Passing Tone** is a note between chord tones that connects them. The chord tones are consonant notes and the passing tone creates tension that resolves. Musical 'tension and release' is an important concept that adds interest and motion to your playing.*

Passing Tones *make for strong bass lines.*

Strive to find your unique voice!

Perdido
Walking Bass Line
More Patterns #2

To more fully internalize:
1. Listen
2. Sing
3. Play

by Bob Sinicrope

WALKING BASS LINE CONSTRUCTION | C Minor Blues

#6.6

Perdido
Walking Bass Line
More Patterns #6

A iim7 V7 chord progression is found in many jazz tunes. When playing a Dominant Seventh, you have an option inserting its iim7 before the Dominant Seventh. Instead of two measures of D7, you could substitute one measure of Am7 to one measure of D7. Letter B of this exercise illustrates this.

The spirit of jazz is the spirit of openness!

To more fully internalize:
1. Listen
2. Sing
3. Play

by Bob Sinicrope

Inspiration, Education, Fun
©2024 SeekingSpirit

WALKING BASS LINE CONSTRUCTION | C Minor Blues

#6.7

This exercise incorporates the concepts presented in this chapter. Have fun creating your own bass lines that use Patterns.

Strive for effortless mastery!

Jazz is the art of thinking out loud!

Perdido
Walking Bass Line
More Patterns - Summary

To more fully internalize:
1. Listen
2. Sing
3. Play

by Bob Sinicrope

Inspiration, Education, Fun
©2024 SeekingSpirit

WALKING BASS LINE CONSTRUCTION | C Minor Blues

CHAPTER 7

Scales

#7.2

*Simplify chord changes. Play **Modal Scales** on the chords in the even numbered measures. Play F Mixolydian (Dominant) scale on the 1st 2 bars and Bb major scale on the next two bars. For the B section play the Mixolydian Scales of those chords.*

Connect with your bass!

Perdido
Walking Bass Line
Scale Pattern #2

To more fully internalize:

1. Listen
2. Sing
3. Play

by Bob Sinicrope

* although the goal of this book is stay within the 1st 5 frets, this bass line neccesitates making an exception.

A1 — F Mixolydian Scale *(in place of Cm7 F7)* | Bb Ionian Scale (Major) *(in place of Bbmaj7 Bb6)*

A2 — F Mixolydian Scale *(in place of Cm7 F7)* | Bb Ionian Scale (Major) *(in place of Bbmaj7 Bb6)*

B — D Mixolydian Scale | G Mixolydian Scale | C Mixolydian Scale | F Mixolydian Scale

A3 — F Mixolydian Scale *(in place of Cm7 F7)* | Bb Ionian Scale (Major) *(in place of Bbmaj7 Bb6)*

Inspiration, Education, Fun
©2024 SeekingSpirit

WALKING BASS LINE CONSTRUCTION | C Minor Blues

#7.3

Some of these scale patterns have an extra note inserted to help place strong pitches (chord tones) on strong beats (1&3) and improve voice leading. This is similar to the Bebop scales.
These patterns also have simplifed chords.

Give it your all in the practice room, at a rehearsal and on the bandstand!

Perdido
Walking Bass Line
Scale Pattern #3

To more fully internalize:
1. Listen
2. Sing
3. Play

by Bob Sinicrope

* although the goal of this book is stay within the 1st 5 frets, this bass line neccesitates making an exception.

WALKING BASS LINE CONSTRUCTION | C Minor Blues

CHAPTER 8

Bass Lines in the style of . . . .

Pops Foster
Walter Page
Milt Hinton
Slam Stewart
Jimmie Blanton
Israel Crosby
George Duvivier
Oscar Pettiford
Percy Heath
Sam Jones
Ray Brown
Red Mitchell
Leroy Vinegar
Andy Simpkins
Paul Chambers
Ron Carter
Charlie Haden
Miroslav Vitous
Bass Line from Backing Track

#8.3

This bass line mimics the style of bassist Milt Hinton. Listen to his recordings to learn about his phrasing and time feel.

Learn about some awesome walking jazz bass players.

Perdido
Walking Bass Line
Bass Line in the style of Milt Hinton

To more fully internalize:
1. Listen
2. Sing
3. Play

by Bob Sinicrope

Inspiration, Education, Fun
©2024 SeekingSpirit

WALKING BASS LINE CONSTRUCTION | C Minor Blues

65

#8.7

This bass line mimics the style of bassist George Duvivier. Listen to his recordings to learn about his phrasing and time feel.

Learn about some awesome walking jazz bass players.

Perdido
Walking Bass Line
Bass Line in the style of George Duvivier

To more fully internalize:
1. Listen
2. Sing
3. Play

by Bob Sinicrope

Inspiration, Education, Fun
©2024 SeekingSpirit

WALKING BASS LINE CONSTRUCTION | C Minor Blues

#8.9

This bass line mimics the style of bassist Percy Heath. Listen to his recordings to learn about his phrasing and time feel.

Learn about some awesome walking jazz bass players.

Perdido
Walking Bass Line
Bass Line in the style of Percy Heath

To more fully internalize:
1. Listen
2. Sing
3. Play

by Bob Sinicrope

Inspiration, Education, Fun
©2024 SeekingSpirit

WALKING BASS LINE CONSTRUCTION | C Minor Blues

#8.10

This bass line mimics the style of bassist Sam Jones. Listen to his recordings to learn about his phrasing and time feel.

Learn about some awesome walking jazz bass players.

Perdido
Walking Bass Line
Bass Line in the style of Sam Jones

To more fully internalize:
1. Listen
2. Sing
3. Play

by Bob Sinicrope

Inspiration, Education, Fun
©2024 SeekingSpirit

#8.11

This bass line mimics the style of bassist Ray Brown. Listen to his recordings to learn about his phrasing and time feel.

Learn about some awesome walking jazz bass players.

Perdido
Walking Bass Line
Bass Line in the style of Ray Brown

To more fully internalize:
1. Listen
2. Sing
3. Play

by Bob Sinicrope

Inspiration, Education, Fun
©2024 SeekingSpirit

WALKING BASS LINE CONSTRUCTION | C Minor Blues

#8.13

This bass line mimics the style of bassist Leroy Vinegar. Listen to his recordings to learn about his phrasing and time feel.

Learn about some awesome walking jazz bass players.

Perdido
Walking Bass Line
Bass Line in the style of Leroy Vinegar

To more fully internalize:
1. Listen
2. Sing
3. Play

by Brian Casey & Bob Sinicrope

Inspiration, Education, Fun
©2024 SeekingSpirit

WALKING BASS LINE CONSTRUCTION | C Minor Blues

#8.15

This bass line mimics the style of bassist Paul Chambers. Listen to his recordings to learn about his phrasing and time feel.

Learn about some awesome walking jazz bass players.

Perdido
Walking Bass Line
Bass Line in the style of Paul Chambers

To more fully internalize:
1. Listen
2. Sing
3. Play

by Bob Sinicrope

Inspiration, Education, Fun
©2024 SeekingSpirit

WALKING BASS LINE CONSTRUCTION | C Minor Blues

#8.18

This is a bass line in the style of Miroslav Vitous. Listen to his recordings to learn about his phrasing and time feel.

Learn about some awesome walking jazz bass players.

Perdido
Walking Bass Line
Bass Line in the style of Miroslav Vitous

To more fully internalize:
1. Listen
2. Sing
3. Play

by Brian Casey

Inspiration, Education, Fun
©2024 SeekingSpirit

WALKING BASS LINE CONSTRUCTION | C Minor Blues

The Sher Music Co. Catalog
VISIT SHERMUSIC.COM FOR MORE INFORMATION AND TO ORDER ONLINE

BEST-SELLING BOOKS BY MARK LEVINE
The Jazz Theory Book
The Jazz Piano Book
Jazz Piano Masterclass: The Drop 2 Book
How To Voice Standards at the Piano

THE WORLD'S BEST FAKE BOOKS
The New Real Book - Vol. 1 - C, Bb and Eb
The New Real Book - Vol. 2 - C, Bb and Eb
The New Real Book - Vol. 3 - C, Bb, Eb & Bass Clef

The Real Easy Book - Vol. 1 - C, Bb, Eb & Bass Clef
The Real Easy Book - Vol. 2 - C, Bb, Eb & Bass Clef
The Real Easy Book - Vol. 3 - C, Bb, Eb & Bass Clef
The Latin Real Easy Book - C, Bb, Eb & Bass Clef
Drum Supplement for Real Easy Book - Vol. 1

The Standards Real Book - C, Bb and Eb
The Latin Real Book - C only
The Real Cool Book - Octet charts from the 1950s
The All-Jazz Real Book - with selected audio
The European Real Book - with selected audio
The Best of Sher Music Real Books - C, Bb & Eb
The World's Greatest Fake Book - C only
Jazz Arrangements of Public Domain Songs
The Yellowjackets Songbook - separate parts

LATIN MUSIC BOOKS
Contemporary Latin Jazz Guitar - Vol. 1&2, by Neff Irizarry
Decoding Afro-Cuban Jazz - by Mauleon & Valdes
The Salsa Guidebook - by Rebeca Mauleõn
101 Montunos - by Rebeca Mauleõn
The Latin Bass Book - by Oscar Stagnaro & Chuck Sher
The Latin Real Book - C only
The True Cuban Bass - by Carlos del Puerto
The Brazilian Guitar Book - by Nelson Faria
Inside the Brazilian Rhythm Section - Faria/Korman
Conga Drummer's Guidebook - by Michael Spiro
Language of the Masters - by Michael Spiro
Introduction to the Conga Drum DVD - by M. Spiro
Afro-Caribbean Grooves for Drumset - JPhi Fanfant
Afro-Peruvian Percussion Ensemble - H. Morales
Flamenco Improvisation - Vol.1-3 by Enrique Vargas
Muy Caliente! - Afro-Cuban Book & Play-Aong audio
Music of the Arará Savalú Cabildo - Galvin & Spiro

DIGITAL FAKE BOOKS
The New Real Book - Vol.1 - C, Bb & Eb
The Digital Standards Songbook - individual songs with lyrics, plus C, Bb, Eb, High Voice & Low Voice
The Digital Real Book (650 songs from all our books)

THE DIGITAL SONGBOOK SERIES
The Kenny Barron Songbook
The Carla Bley Songbook
The Tom Harrell Songbook
The Oscar Hernandez Songbook
The Alan Pasqua Songbook
The Horace Silver Songbook
The Steve Swallow Songbook
The Ralph Towner Songbook
The Wayne Wallace Songbook
The Kenny Werner Songbook
The Randy Brecker Songbook
The Larry Dunlap Songbook
The Barry Finnerty Songbook
The Benny Golson Songbook
The Steve Khan Songbook
The Doug Morton Songbook
The Andy Narell Songbook
The Enrico Pieranunzi Songbook
The Dave Tull Songbook
The Denny Zeitlin Songbook

FOR STUDENT MUSICIANS
The Real Easy Book - Vol. 1 - C, Bb, Eb & Bass Clef
The Real Easy Book - Vol. 2 - C, Bb, Eb & Bass Clef
The Real Easy Book - Vol. 3 - C, Bb, Eb & Bass Clef
The Latin Real Easy Book - C, Bb, Eb & Bass Clef
Drum Supplement for Real Easy Book - Vol. 1
The Blues Scales - C, Bb, Eb, Bass Clef & Guitar
Rhythm First! - C, Bb, Eb & Bass Clef - by Tom Kamp
Guitarist's Introduction to Jazz - by Randy Vincent
Walking Bassics - by Ed Fuqua
Foundation Exercises for Bass - by Chuck Sher

CDs
Poetry+Jazz: A Magical Marriage - by Chuck Sher
Play-Along CDs for The New Real Book - Vol.1
The Latin Real Book Sampler CD

Sher Music Co.
JAZZ METHOD BOOKS
available in both print & digital forms

GUITAR
Jazz Guitar Voicings: The Drop 2 Book
   - Randy Vincent
Three-Note Voicings and Beyond - Randy Vincent
Line Games - Randy Vincent
Jazz Guitar Soloing: The Cellular Approach
   - Randy Vincent
The Guitarist's Introduction to Jazz - Randy Vincent
Contemporary Latin Jazz Guitar, Vol. 1&2 - Neff Irizarry
The Jimmy Raney Book - Jimmy and Jon Raney

PIANO
The Jazz Piano Book - Mark Levine
Jazz Piano Masterclass: The Drop 2 Book - M. Levine
How To Voice Standards at the Piano - Mark Levine
An Approach to Comping - Vol. 1 - Jeb Patton
An Approach to Comping - Vol. 2 - Jeb Patton
Introduction to Jazz Piano: A Deep Dive - Jeb Patton
Playing for Singers - Mike Greensill
Wisdom of the Hand - Marius Nordal
The Jazz Solos of Chick Corea - Peter Sprague

SAXOPHONE
The Practice Notebooks of Michael Brecker
The Jazz Saxophone Book - Tim Armacost
Logic and Critical Thinking in Jazz Improvisation
   - Vincent Herring

VOICE
The Digital Standards Songbook - individual songs
   with lyrics, plus C, Bb, Eb, High Voice & Low Voice
The Jazz Singer's Guidebook - David Berkman

DRUMS
Syncopation Companion - Bryan Bowman
Inner Drumming - George Marsh
Drum Supplement for Real Easy Book Vol.1 - Alan Hall
Afro-Caribbean Grooves for Drumset - JPhi Fanfant

BASS
The Improvisor's Bass Method - Chuck Sher
Concepts for Bass Soloing - Marc Johnson & C. Sher
Walking Bassics - Ed Fuqua
Foundation Exercises for Bass - Chuck Sher
Walking Bass Line Construction - Bob Sinicrope
   F Blues, Bb Blues and C minor Blues
Bass Foundations - Chuck Israels

*Sign up for our monthly discount newsletter
by writing shermuse@sonic.net*

JAZZ THEORY AND HARMONY
The Jazz Theory Book - Mark Levine
The Jazz Harmony Book - David Berkman
Forward Motion - Hal Galper
Metaphors for the Musician - Randy Halberstadt
Minor is Major! - Dan Greenblatt
Rhythm Changes Guide - Lukas Gabric
Jazz Scores and Analysis - Vol.1 - Richard Lawn
Jazz Scores and Analysis - Vol. 2 - Richard Lawn
The Blues Scales - C, Bb, Eb, Bass Clef & Guitar
   - Dan Greenblatt
Logic and Critical Thinking in Jazz Improvisation
   - Vincent Herring
Major is Harmonic - Randy Vincent

PRACTICE GUIDES
The Practice Notebooks of Michael Brecker
Jazz Musician's Guide to Creative Practicing
   - David Berkman
The Serious Jazz Practice Book - Barry Finnerty
The Serious Jazz Book II - Barry Finnerty
Building Solo Lines from Cells - Randy Vincent
365 Days of Practice - Rick Margitza
Bob Mover Jazz Lexicon - 2nd edtion - Bob Mover
   - Bass & Treble Clef versions

EAR TRAINING
The Real Easy Ear Training Book - Roberta Radley
Reading, Writing and Rhythmetic - Roberta Radley

TRUMPET
New Orleans Trumpet - Jim Thornton
Modern Etudes for Solo Trumpet - Cameron Pearce

RHYTHM SECTION GUIDES
Essential Grooves - Moretti, Stagnaro & Nicholl
Inside the Brazilian Rhythm Section - Nelson Faria
   & Cliff Korman
The Salsa Guidebook - Rebeca Mauleón
Decoding Afro-Cuban Jazz - Mauleón & Valdes

BILINGUAL OR LIBROS EN ESPANOL
101 Montunos - Rebeca Mauleón
Muy Caliente! - Afro-Cuban Book & Play-Along
El Libro del Jazz Piano - Mark Levine
The Latin Real Book - C only

MISCELLANEOUS
Method for Chromatic Harmonica - Max de Aloe
Jazz Songs for the Student Violinist
   - Kevin Mitchell & Joanne Keefe